INVERNESS REMEMBERED
IV

Published By
New Century Publishing Group

New Century
Publishing Group

The Inverness Courier

Edited by Willie Morrison

The photographs in this book were sourced with the generous help of the people named below, who were kind enough to respond to our appeal for fascinating reminders of Inverness in bygone days, and from Highland Council Photographic Archive. Every effort has been made to ensure the information used is as accurate as possible.

John M Allan	Wilma MacGregor	J A MacLean
Sheila Burnett	W Milne	Stewart MacLennan
Allan Cameron	W A McAdam	Christine McLoughlin
Iain Cameron	Mrs Alma MacDonald	Mrs P MacPherson
Hamish Campbell	Angus MacDonald	A MacRae
A Chisholm	Charlie Macdonald	Ted Murdoch
Mr and Mrs Chisholm	Fiona MacDonald	Margaret Murphy
Peter Chisholm	Iain MacDonald	Mary Nairne
M B Corrance	John MacDonald	Philip Owen
Sandra Delamere	Mrs M MacDonald	Alister Paterson
Dorothy Evans	Rosemary MacGregor	Mrs G Price
James Fraser	Hester MacInnes	Alan Ross
Miss M Fraser	Betty Mackay	Mrs P Ross
Irene Gillespie	Duncan MacKay	Willie Shand
Ena Gordon	Mrs June Mackay	Christine Smith
David Gray	Mrs E Mackay	Mrs N C Stewart
Olive Gunn	Christine Mackenzie	Douglas Taylor
J C Hay	Sally Mackenzie	J Wemyss
Freda Irvine	Mrs V MacKinnon	S Williamson

CONTENTS

INTRODUCTION

THE appeal for interesting photographs for this year's volume of Inverness Remembered yielded a really bumper crop, from a great variety of sources.

Our thanks to all who sent in their treasured snaps for publication.

Such has been the response, that while we've used as many as we could, we must, for the sake of variety keep a good number for future volumes.

This year, given the character of pictures submitted, we have probably concentrated more on events within living memory than those in the distant past, though we have not forgotten our city's Victorian and Edwardian photographic heritage.

Perhaps the message that springs from the pages of Inverness Remembered IV more than anything else is the pace of change over the past half-century, much of it sadly for the worse, especially in the 1960s, when the scramble for easy pickings and in the case of the planning authorities, for increased rateable values, resulted in an epidemic of Soviet-style glass-and-concrete buildings mushrooming along the riverside.

Turn over the pages and see some of the buildings the present Bridge Street, Bank Street and Church Street developments have replaced, and make your own comparisons and judgements.

Soulless developers would doubtless argue that the Museum-cum-Crofters' Commission complex was of more economic value to the town than the Workmen's Club, the handsome complex of flats overlooking the river known as Castle Tolmie and other buildings it replaced. But what of the aesthetic value? That apparently didn't figure in the lemming rush of the 1960s to tear down the heart of old Inverness.

Copyright of the Highland Photographic Archive, Inverness Museum and Gallery

The old Suspension Bridge was certainly not suited to modern traffic. But did it have to go? Could not some of it have been saved for posterity?

Are the former Highlands and Islands Development Board headquarters-cum-Littlewoods slab, now largely converted into flats, and the nearby Ramada Jarvis Hotel, buildings of beauty and architectural merit, or excrescences more in keeping with a 1960s Glasgow slum clearance scheme? Their beauty, surely, must only have been in the eye of the profiteer.

Sadly, it seems, another surge of New Brutalism seems to be making progress, if one considers a scattering of carbuncles which have sprung up around the town in recent years, or if a number of recent planning applications reach full term.

To add variety, we have included many photographs of people at work or at play in a great variety of situations. We hope they will rekindle happy memories for those of a certain age, who were young a generation or two ago, but who still enjoy healthy anecdotage, and that they will be appreciated as well as informative to the present younger generation.

We have received some interesting feedback on photos in last year's issue on which we had little information. Robert McPhee, of Darnaway Road, tells us that the house which the pretty bride on Page 15 is leaving for her wedding ceremony is now his. She was Catherine Black, daughter of John D M Black, a former headmaster of Merkinch Public School, and she married Jack Reid. The couple lived in Africa for many years. Catherine's father built the house in 1935/36.

Meanwhile, Gladys Sanderson informs us that the Industry House in Church Street, featured on Page 59, where she obtained her first job as a junior assistant in 1955, at a weekly wage of £1 12s 9d – £1.64 in today's money – was owned by a Mr Morris, who also owned The Fashion Salon in Union Street.

"He was a big man, who always left a trail of cigar smoke behind him," recalls Mrs Sanderson, who adds that by the time she started there, the shop mostly stocked outdoor fashions, evening and wedding dresses, and competed keenly with Charles Morgan's shop across the road.

How Times Have Changed

CATTLE IN BANK STREET 1930s

Long after the motor-car reached Inverness, cattle were often herded through its streets to the marts, as this photo shows. These beasts, with a posse of cattlemen and an intelligent collie, are seen passing the taxi rank in Bank Street. The car nearest to the camera, a Rover P3, and others beside it, indicate that this was taken in the late 1930s, or perhaps just after the war. Towards the end of the 19th century, ordinary markets were held in Inverness every Tuesday and Friday, while livestock markets were held on Fridays following the formerly important Muir of Ord markets. Two firms of agricultural auctioneers were established around this time – Hamilton's Auction Marts Ltd and Macdonald Fraser & Co Ltd.

Inverness became an important centre for the sale of stock, while Muir of Ord decreased rapidly in importance. Today, the wheel has turned full circle, as the Highlands' main mart has returned to Ross-shire, at Dingwall, while the Inverness marts are no more.

CAMERON HIGHLANDERS GO TO WAR

These Territorial Army soldiers of the 4th Battalion Queen's Own Cameron Highlanders are seen marching along Academy Street, Inverness, towards the railway station, in August 1914, after being mobilised for war. They were sent briefly to Cromarty, to protect the naval base in the Cromarty Firth, before being posted to Bedford for further training with the Seaforth and Cameron Brigade. The 960-strong battalion arrived in France in February 1915 and in its first major action, an attack on Neuve Chapelle, suffered 140 casualties. The two officers in the picture are believed to be Lieutenant W J Shaw (left) and Second Lieutenant J D M Black, who both, amazingly, survived the war. The khaki spats seen here proved impractical in the trenches and were replaced by puttees.

THE COKE OVEN

This rare photo from late Victorian days shows the coke oven, apparently owned by the Highland Railway, where old notes of the locally-owned Caledonian Bank were destroyed after they had become too tattered for further use. Presumably the large basket in the picture was being carried out empty, after disgorging used notes into the oven. The Caledonian Banking Company, formed in 1838, served Inverness and much of the North of Scotland. It had its first office on Castle Street in Inverness until the company's headquarters were built on High Street, in 1849. Early in its history, the Caledonian Bank employed the firm W H Lizars & Co to print specially designed banknotes. The notes were unique in that they included a Gaelic inscription on them which translated as "Land of Mountains, Glens, and Heroes". The notes also incorporated a view of the River Ness and Inverness Castle on them. Later in the 19th century, when the notes were printed by George Waterston & Sons, advanced overlay printing techniques were used as prevention against counterfeiting, a technique unique for a 19th century note. In 1907, the Caledonian Bank was absorbed by the Bank of Scotland, which itself now faces an uncertain future.

NORTHERN MEETING PARK SCOUT RALLY

This shows the 1912 Boy Scout Rally at the Northern Meeting Park, Inverness. The inspecting officer was Alfred Donald Mackintosh of Mackintosh, Boy Scout Commissioner for Inverness-shire and Lord Lieutenant of the county. During the event the Hon Ida Merry of Belladrum, a supporter of the Kiltarlity Troop, was presented with a Thanks Badge by Inverness Scouts under Scoutmaster Paulin and Assistant Scoutmaster Rhind. The Boy Scout Movement was founded by Sir Robert Baden-Powell in August 1907.

ROYAL INSURANCE COMPANY
This 1953 photograph shows the office and staff of the Royal Insurance Company at Queensgate in Inverness.

ATC FLOAT
Members of the local Air Training Corps squadron, with their home-made flight of fancy about the future of aviation, take part in a parade at Clachnacuddin Park in the 1950s. The Albion lorries used for the floats are those of Inverness haulage contractor John Robertson. This photo is from the Jimmy Nairn and Son Collection in Highland Council's Am Baile archive. Jimmy Nairn himself served as an officer in the newly-formed Inverness branch of the ATC during World War II, and used his amazing electrical and mechanical aptitude to create training gadgets unavailable to other such units. His older son, Jimmy Jnr, as a youth a founder member of Inverness ATC, later trained as an RAF pilot, before returning to Inverness to run a photographic shop with his brother Lewis.

EARLY SUPERMARKET

One of the first self service style stores in Inverness was the Scottish Midland Co-operative Society store at 59-65 Church Street, pictured here in 1953. These photos, presumably taken for advertising purposes by David Whyte Studios, demonstrate the last word, over half a century ago, in modern retail thinking. The Church Street Co-op still remains at the same site, though it has long since been dwarfed by superstores on the town's perimeter.

GORDON'S GARAGE

Local businessman George Gordon set up a state of the art garage called Gordon's Garage in Muirfield Road in the 1950s. It flourished for around 40 years, until eventually knocked down to make way for a complex of flats. Pictured with a bevy of cars of half a century ago are from left: George himself, his wife Phyllis, mechanic Kenny Malcolm and Billy Ferguson. The cars from left, all British-made, and top of their respective ranges, are: Austin A90 Westminster, Sunbeam Rapier, Hillman Californian and Jaguar Mk VII. See also pages 57 and 89.

REMAINS OF NESS ISLANDS PAVILION

Many Invernessians and visitors will recall the pavilion in the Ness Islands, formerly used in summer months to stage open air Scottish-themed concerts for tourists, and other events. This picture was taken on a dismal day in 1981, shortly before it was demolished. The two boys in the photo showing the covered stage are Iain (right) and Calum Morrison, who then lived in Darris Road. See also the pictures od dancers in the Ness Islands on page 18.

BURNETTS' VAN

George Owen, proudly taking delivery of his new Burnetts' van in January, 1956. The Albion Claymore was supplied by Inverness Motor Co Ltd and became the latest addition to a fleet belonging to the famous Burnetts' Bakery.

INVERNESS FIRE ENGINE 1949
The firemen showing these little boys their Dennis fire engine are, from left, Angus MacLean, Gordon Taylor and Willie Shand. Willie, now 84 and retired in Nairn, ended a distinguished career in the fire service as the brigade's firemaster. He recalls that the fire engine, reminiscent of the Dinky Toy version so beloved of boys of that period, had been registered either AST 14 or AST 17, shortly before the war, and boasted a 50ft wooden wheeled escape ladder, part of which is visible in the picture.

BODICE MAKERS, YOUNG & CHAPMAN CIRCA 1909
This group of young ladies, photographed less than a century ago, pursued a now long-vanished trade – that of bodice-maker – in Young & Chapman's store in Union Street. The store was later owned by Benzie & Miller, Arnott's & House of Fraser, before being sub-divided in recent years to accommodate a number of smaller businesses. Chief bodice-maker at that time was Helen MacLennan from Tore, seated front row, centre, grandmother of June Mackay who sent this photo in.

LAST OF THE LAMPLIGHTERS, CIRCA 1950

This historic photo was taken around 1950, as the burgh council's "leeries" or lamplighters marched up from their base at Castle Wynd with their lighting poles, prior to undertaking their very last shift before the town's street lights were switched to automatic ignition by a control clock. Before the war the lamplighters also formed a part-time fire-fighting unit to assist the full-time Inverness Fire Brigade, based at Fraser Park. Frozen in time, from the front, were: William MacKenzie, Alexander Ross, Tom Taylor, Ian Mellis, Donald Robertson, Alexander Lumsden, unidentified and Roderick Mackay. The picture was taken by Sandy McLaren, who for many years operated a branch of his family firm, Star Photos, in Inverness. Mobilised on the outbreak of hostilities in 1939 as a TA officer, Sandy became an official war photographer, with the rank of captain, and for a time personal photographer to General Bernard Montgomery in the Western Desert, until seriously wounded by a landmine. He left his remarkable collection of war photos to Inverness British Legion Club, of which he remained a member until his death.

FISHING BOATS IN THE CALEDONIAN CANAL 1932

These two Yarmouth-registered fishing boats, possibly herring drifters, were snapped in the Caledonian Canal in 1932, after coming south from Inverness on their way to the fertile west coast fishing grounds. The location appears to be the lock at the north end of Loch Oich, a few miles south of Fort Augustus.

Party Times and Nights Out

POST OFFICE STAFF DANCE
These were members of Inverness Post Office staff, photographed in the ballroom of the Caledonian Hotel in August 1960. The ballroom, opened in 1938 by superstar Anna Neagle, was a mecca for thousands of local dancers for nearly a generation, before being demolished with the rest of the hotel in 1966.

STATION HOTEL
The Station Hotel's magnificent staircase was the scene – as it was for so many group photos across the generations – for this picture of some members of Inverness Motor Trade Association and friends enjoying their annual ball in the early 1960s.

SCOTTISH COUNTRY DANCE GROUP
Snapped here in the Caledonian Hotel ballroom around 1960 were, from left: Marlene McDowall, Jack Ross, Olive Fraser, Jim Murray, Catherine Munro, unidentified.

BURGH POLICE BALL 1963
Members of Inverness Burgh Police force are pictured here in 1963 tripping the light fantastic at their annual ball, in of course, the ballroom of the Old Caledonian Hotel.

HIDB PARTY

This Highlands and Islands Development Board Christmas party photo was taken in 1970. Front, third from right, is the board's new chairman, bearded cigar-smoking Peter Ustinov-lookalike Sir Andrew Gilchrist, a post which he held for six years. Also in the photograph are board members Lt Col Hector MacKenzie, war hero and distillery boss from Inness, front, right, Shetland-born former Merchant Navy seaman Prophet Smith, front, third from left, and board secretary Iain MacAskill, second row from rear, right.

INVERNESSIANS IN THE BIG CITY

Although this photo was taken around 1962 at a Hallowe'en party in a flat at Ruskin Place, Glasgow, most of those pictured are contemporary Inverness students. Photographer Willie Morrison from Sutherland, himself a student and later an Inverness-based journalist, took it using the 10-second delayed action function on a tripod-mounted Kodak Retinette IIB camera, and rushed into the group to sprawl on the floor on the right. A slightly bewildered-looking Ewan Lawson – son of late Inverness-shire deputy education director Alan B Lawson – is looking at him in surprise. Ewan's fiancee Maureen Fleming, also from Inverness, is just behind him, while on his other side is another of a quintet of bonny Inverness lassies, Eileen Mackenzie, now Mackinnon and living in Skye. Ewan, a fine pianist, and Maureen married and emigrated to Australia, and although now parted, both still live there and are grandparents. Looking at Eileen, is another of the quintet, Jean Smith, now Macdonald and living in Wick. The bespectacled lad centre, front, is James Sydie from Inverness. He emigrated to Canada but sadly died some years ago. The four from left are Gus Beudall, Maureen Balfour (with basket on her head), whom he married, but who has also passed on, Gus's sister Margaret, who also went to Australia, and Isabel Johnstone. The lad at the very back is Willie's brother David, who later worked for the Highlands and Islands Development Board and lived for several years in Inverness. The bearded young man behind Willie is Rodney Mackenzie, originally from Lochinver, Sutherland now living in Avoch, and father of four of the Highlands' finest female singers, including two National Mod gold medallists. The girl behind the mask is Hilda Ross, from Portsoy. We haven't been able to identify the two young men beside David Morrison.

FIRE SERVICE CHILDREN'S PARTY 1977
Children of Northern Area Fire Brigade employee[s] are pictured here at their Christmas party [in] 1977. Firemaster Willie Shand acted as Santa.

DANCERS IN THE NESS ISLANDS 1959
Highland dancers in the Ness Islands Pavilion 1959, from left: Margaret Fraser Alison Ross, Eleanor Macrae and Olive Fraser, who submitted this picture. Olive, now Mrs Gunn, and her colleagues, were keen members of Florence Martin's dancing class. The auditorium, used in the summer months for many, mainly Scottish-themed shows aimed mainly at tourists, was finally demolished in 1981. (See also the picture of the remains of the Ness Islands Pavilion on page 8)

JIMMY SHAND AND JACK RADCLIFFE AT PLAYHOUSE CINEMA, EARLY 1960S

Inverness Scottish country dancers appeared with top national entertainers at this live show in the Playhouse Cinema in the early 1960s, when accordion maestro Jimmy Shand (right) and Scots comedian Jack Radcliffe topped the bill. Among the dancers, from left, were: Alex Wiseman, Olive Fraser, Hugh MacKenzie, Irene Whyte, Eleanor Macrae, Margaret Fraser, Bob Morton, Catherine Munro, Vi Connell, Charlie Berry. The much-loved Playhouse was occasionally used for staging shows, in addition to its primary purpose. It burned down, sadly, in March 1972.

DONALD PEERS AT THE EMPIRE THEATRE 1963

One of Britain's earliest pop idols, Donald Peers of A Babbling Brook fame, had moved on to become a TV personality with his own show, when he was photographed scanning a copy of the Highland News with this bevy of local dancers at the Empire Theatre in 1963. Born in Wales to a staunchly religious family in 1908, Donald Peers eked out a living as a contract painter for many years before he found fame as a singer. He died in 1973, aged 65, his death almost certainly hastened by an accident on stage in Australia, in which he broke his back. The girls in the picture are, from left: Rosemary MacGregor, Angela Paterson, Violet Ross, Margaret Firth and Rose Mackintosh. Margaret Firth, a dance teacher in Inverness for decades, died earlier this year.

TELEPHONISTS' CHILDREN'S CHRISTMAS PARTY 1956
The youngsters in this photo were enjoying a Christmas party held in 1956 by Inverness telephonists for their children. The event was organised by Charlie MacDonald, the supervisor, who sent this picture.

LMS GIRLS' SWIMMING TEAM 1953
An evening in Tahiti was the theme adopted by these members of the LMS Girls' Swimming Team, when photographed in 1953. Rear, from left: Margo Anderson, "Mike" Mackenzie, Christine Kelly, Isabel Ross, Rosemarie Anderson; front, from left: Liz Mackenzie, Sandra Whyte, Jean Livingstone, Claire Hepburn, Maureen Smart. Recalls Sandra Whyte, now Lea: "It was a display we put on at a gala called 'Evening in Tahiti'. We were supposed to be the hula girls. Willie Allen came up the pool in a canoe with the coloured lights on the water and there we were at the shallow end doing a hula dance to the music! Those were the days."

THOMSON & BROWN BROTHERS STAFF DANCE CIRCA 1949
Nearly sixty years have passed since this happy group of Thomson & Brown Brothers met in the Columba Hotel, Inverness, in 1949 or 1950 to hold their annual staff dance. Thomson & Brown, now Brown Brothers, was at that time located in Eastgate, next to the Albert Hotel, across the road from the blacksmith's smiddy, but later moved to Castle Street. Rear, from left, are: Mrs Macbean, Mrs Legge, Jimmy Legge, Cath - , John Wilson, Helen Bruce, Alex Wilson, Pat Petrie, Danny Moir, Duncan Mackay, Moira Macdonald; front, from left; Jim Macbean, Joyce Munro, Madge - , Bill Robertson (manager), Mrs Robertson, Frances Gordon, Mrs Moir.

Buildings And Views You May Recognise

AMONG the many pictures submitted by members of the public for this year's volume of Inverness Remembered were several interesting slides, taken between the late 1950s and 1972, from retired builder Hamish Campbell, whose firm was involved in many of the changes which took place in the burgh centre in that period. They are reproduced on this and the following 10 pages.

Perhaps Mr Campbell's own most significant personal contribution towards the preservation of something worthwhile of old Inverness was the salvation and tasteful renovation of 17th Century Dunbar's Hospital and adjoining Bow Court, still in everyday use as flats.

INVERNESS LATE 1950s – CASTLE TOLMIE
Despite being in good condition, Castle Tolmie, a handsome complex of flats, designed in late Victorian times by well-known local architect Robert Carruthers, to replace an earlier edifice of the same name, was demolished in the early 1960s to make way for the concrete monstrosity which became the first headquarters of the Highlands and Island Development Board. It is pictured here a few years before demolition. The cars in the photo are, from left, a Ford Zodiac Mk2, an early 1950s Hillman Minx, a Vauxhall with an AST registration plate, indicating that it was delivered just before or very shortly after the war, and a mid-1930s Ford 8.

BANK LANE NOV 1965

All the buildings seen in this 1965 shot of Bank Lane were demolished shortly within the next few years, apart from the Inverness Courier building, which the newspaper's doughty editor and proprietor Eveline Barron resolutely refused to sell to get-rich quick developers. It remains as a solitary, and now hopefully permanent monument, to what the city centre ought to have looked like.

BEHIND BRIDGE STREET PRIOR TO DEMOLITION

A photo from 1963, taken shortly before the south side of Bridge Street was demolished to make way for the dismal glass and concrete development which replaced it. Note the spires of St Columba High, the Free North and Old High Churches, which happily all still survive, and the "German" gasometer, long demolished.

BRIDGE STREET LAST STAGES OF DEMOLITION 1963
A crane belonging to building contractor Campbell prepares to push over the last remnant of the south side of old Bridge Street, the frontage of the Workmen's Club in 1963.

BRIDGE STREET AFTER DEMOLITION 1963
The demolition of the south side of Bridge Street had been completed when this photo was taken in autumn 1963. Picturesque Queen Mary's House and the building adjoining would survive for a further six years, until demolished to make way for another glass and concrete monstrosity to house the now defunct Littlewood's Store and the ever-expanding quango, the Highlands and Islands Development Board. The Gellions pub, thankfully, has survived, but the old Caledonian Hotel, behind this block, was demolished two years later.

RIDGE STREET AFTER DEMOLITION OCT 1963

nis photo, from October 1963, shows contractors starting to prepare foundations for the new Bridge Street redevelopment.

RIDGE STREET JULY 1968

n completion in 1965, this Stalinesque concrete development on Bridge Street housed the Burgh Library and Museum, the Crofters' Commission and overlooking the River Ness, e first Highlands and Islands Development Board offices. The Crofters' Commission remains in the block, as does the museum, but the library has moved to Farraline Park, hile the HIDB's successor, Highlands and Islands Enterprise, has survived a couple of moves and is now based at Cowan House, on the city's eastern perimeter.

ote on the ground floor Lipton's supermarket, now long gone, and the "shops to let" signs on the floor above. The series of small shops on that floor never found many takers lease, nor much business, and were eventually converted to form the present tourist office. Note the policeman on point duty directing traffic into Church Street, now long nce closed off to vehicles from Bridge Street.

CHURCH STREET NOV 1965
Church Street is seen here in November 1965, with the entrance to the old Caledonian Hotel still in evidence, although the building was even then being prepared ┃ demolition and redevelopment.

FIRST YELLOW BOX JULY 1975
This photo from July 1975 shows one of the first criss-crossed yellow traffic-control boxes in the north, at the junction of Bridge Street and Bank Street. Note that parking at right angles to the street was still permitted in the latter.

DEMOLITION OF QUEEN MARY'S HOUSE 1969

Demolition work progressing at the site of the former Queen Mary's House, on the corner of Bank Street and Bridge Street. The old house, latterly used as a wine merchant's premises, had stood on the site of an earlier house in which Mary Queen of Scots had stayed, during a visit to Inverness four centuries before.

FRIARS' STREET JULY 1972
This was the view looking south along Friars' Street in July 1972, towards the Old High Church, before the Telephone Exchange on the left was extended northwards, ar
the cottages on the right were mostly demolished, to make way for similar-looking modern houses.

HIGH STREET JULY 1975
Inverness High Street looking east from the balcony of the new Bridge Street development. Buildings in the picture, from left, include the Bank of Scotland, the rebu
Woolworth's store, the Highland Club and the Northern Hotel. The cars the traffic warden in the foreground might have dealt with in the summer of 1975 were still large
British-built, like the Mini and the Ford Cortina Mk1 heading west down the street.

TEMPORARY NESS BRIDGE LATE 1950s

The temporary bridge across the River Ness stood alongside the 1855 Suspension Bridge for many years, in a bid to relieve the pressure of traffic, and latterly, while the new bridge was under construction, carried it all. The presence of a red-capped military policeman at the bottom left-hand corner of the picture indicates either the imminent arrival or passing of a military parade. The windows on the right belong to a handsome block of flats known as Castle Tolmie.

NEW NESS BRIDGE CONSTRUCTION

The new Ness Bridge, opened in 1961, was still under construction a few months before when this photo was taken from close to Inverness Castle. The building in the right hand bottom corner would bite the dust within the next three years, to make way for the "innovative" glass and concrete structure still defacing the south end of Bridge Street.

LAST DAYS OF THE MUCH LOVED CALEY

One of the buildings most missed by local people in the wake of the mass demolitions of the mid-1960s was the old Caledonian Hotel, on a commanding site between Church Street and Bank Street.

Opened in 1780, it was knocked down shortly after this photo was taken, and replaced in 1967 by a featureless "luxury" modernist structure, of a design perhaps more appropriate to a contemporary Glasgow council housing scheme.

Even the name Caledonian Hotel vanished three decades later, to be renamed the Ramada Jarvis, although Invernessians often still refer to it unconsciously as "The Caley".

Although scarcely an architectural wonder, the old Caley nonetheless had a

istinct character and presence, as these photos, taken in November 1965, emonstrate. It was at that time being prepared for its eventual fate and eing stripped of its fittings.

he Masonic symbol on the wall at the right (opposite page) indicates omething of the Caley's origins, when in 1766 St John's (Kilwinning) Lodge f Freemasons decided to build a Masonic lodge on the site.

en years later the lodge's members decided to turn it into a hotel, ncorporating their own meeting rooms, at a cost of £1,800. The first enant, John Ettles, took up his lease of what was originally called the New Hotel, at an annual rent of £50, in 1780.

xtended progressively in 1803, 1859 and 1881, it increased in popularity nder succeeding tenants, and with the coming of the railways in mid-19th entury, was leased to the Caledonian Railway Company, from which it ook its later name.

One of its most notable managers, Sutherland-born Frank Steven, himself an enthusiastic Freemason, eventually bought the building from St John's Lodge in 1930, and sold it on his retirement in 1936 to the newly formed North British Hotels Ltd, a company set up by local solicitor Robert Wotherspoon, of MacAndrew & Jenkins.

The new owners embarked on an ambitious series of improvements and alterations, including the construction of a new ballroom, opened by screen superstar Anna Neagle in March 1938, when 288 couples are said to have taken to the floor for the inaugural dance. The ballroom, which immediately became popular with local dancers, also saw the arrival of the burgh's first resident dance band, Bert Valentine and his Versatile Orchestra.

Sadly all of that was to change within the span of a generation. The ballroom's latter-day replacement, the function room of the present building, was opened on May 26, 1967, by a C-List, mini-skirted celebrity called Susan Maughan, whose song Bobby's Girl had reached the charts five years before.

**OLD CALEDONIAN HOTEL
NOVEMBER 1965**
This view of the Church Street entrance of the Caley was also taken in November 1965, as the hotel was being prepared for demolition. The van outside belongs to A Goodfellow, Tarmac & Demolition Contractor, Perth, and the trailer to the North of Scotland Hydro Electric Co Ltd.

REAR OF CALEDONIAN HOTEL NOV 1965

The rear shell of the Caledonian Hotel is pictured here as internal stripping is taking place inside, prior to demolition of the outer walls. The much-loved 1938 ballroom is clear visible. Among the vehicles parked outside the hotel in the picture above are two BM 1100s, a Vauxhall Viva Mk1, a Mini, an Austin A35 van and an early Morris 1000 – c manufactured in Britain.

MACKENZIE MOTORS, TOMNAHURICH STREET, JULY 1968

This was the first showroom set up in Tomnahurich Street, over 40 years ago, by car salesman the late Donald Mackenzie, after he decided to branch out on his own. Som years later the burgeoning business moved across the street to the premises vacated by Rossleigh Motors, and later, by then a main Fiat agent, to the Longman Industri Estate, where it still thrives. This photo of the fledgling venture was taken in July 1968.

DUFF STREET, LATE 19TH CENTURY

This group of women and children was pictured outside a derelict house on Duff Street, on the west side of the Ness, which in the latter part of the 19th Century was in some parts very run-down and in the grip of considerable poverty. It would be classed, by today's standards as a "deprived area". By the 1900s, the thatched roofs in the photograph were being replaced by slates, and gas street lighting was being introduced.

E REID'S SHOP

This little newsagent's shop, now long demolished to make way for roadworks, was located at the north end of Academy Street at its confluence with Church Street and Chapel Street. It probably dates to shortly after World War II, as a Herald poster outside announces 1,250,000 ACRES FOR JEWISH REFUGEES. A Daily Record poster states HIGHLAND DROWNING TRAGEDY. In the background, in Church Street, is a corner of the former Technical School, demolished in the 1970s.

EASIEPHIT

Greenlees & Sons Footwear Ltd in Academy Street, was for many years a supplier of products by Easiephit Footwear Ltd. By the 1950s, when this photo was taken, Easiephit had taken top billing over the firm's own name.

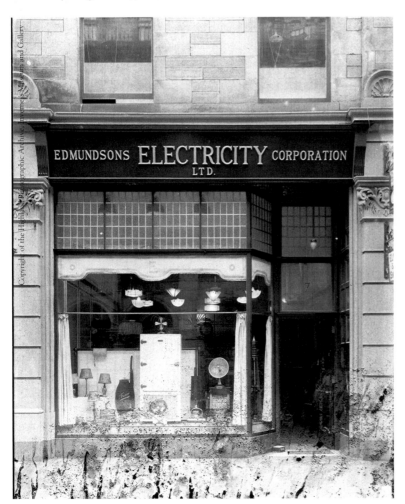

EDMUNDSONS

Edmundson's Electricity Corporation Ltd, a couple of generations ago located at 7 Queengate, was a very advanced supplier for its time, which is perhaps why it is one of very few local businesses of that time still to exist, although it has long since shifted its premises to the Longman Industrial Estate. In addition to selling the usual run of domestic appliances, such as the Thor vacuum cleaner in the window, it advertised in an Inverness guide book, published around 1935, diesel-powered home generators.

ETTLES HOTEL

This photo, stated by the Highland Council archive Am Baile to be of the Ettles Hotel in Old Bridge Street, poses a mystery. The first tenant of the Old Caledonian Hotel in 1780 was a John Ettles, but this is certainly not part of the Caledonian. "Mr Ettles' Hotel" was said to have been visited by Robert Burns and his schoolteacher companion Willie Nicol, on the poet's third tour of Scotland in 1787, while the following year it hosted the 13 gentlemen founders of the new Northern Meeting Society, but surely that was more likely to have been the Caledonian. Did Mr Ettles run another hotel before he took over the tenancy of the Caley? From the attire of the little girl and the woman walking up the street, this picture seems to be from the inter-war years, despite the grim Victorian appearance of their settings. The plaque faintly visible on the corner of a building on the other side of the road appears to advertise yet another hotel – perhaps the Gellions, once lauded by the "world's worst bad poet", William Topaz McGonagall, and still to the fore.

FRASER'S STONE WORKS

This group, pictured outside Fraser's Stone Works on Academy Street, dates from around 1900. Behind the Stone Works are the premises of Stewart & Maclean, house carpenters. The wooden sign in the photograph also points the way to the Granite Works in Queensgate, opposite the Post Office.

GARAGE WITH OLD VAUXHALL

This photo by Jimmy Nairn shows Benson's garage and filling station in Montague Row. The houses in the background are on Tomnahurich Street. The car nearest the camera is a 1930s Vauxhall, and the others are even older, but the design of the nearest petrol pump indicates that the photo was taken in the 1950s.

HUGH MACKENZIE & SON

Hugh Mackenzie & Son, located at 52 & 54 Baron Taylor's Street, described itself in an guide book advert from the 1930s as being "bespoke boot and brogue makers", and "agents for Kenzie, Bective, Excelsior, Nil-simile, Lightfoot and the famous Start-Rite shoes for children". This photo was clearly taken the following decade, as the display in the window, rather than showing the firm's wares, celebrates the 1947 wedding of Lieutenant Philip Mountbatten to Princess Elizabeth.

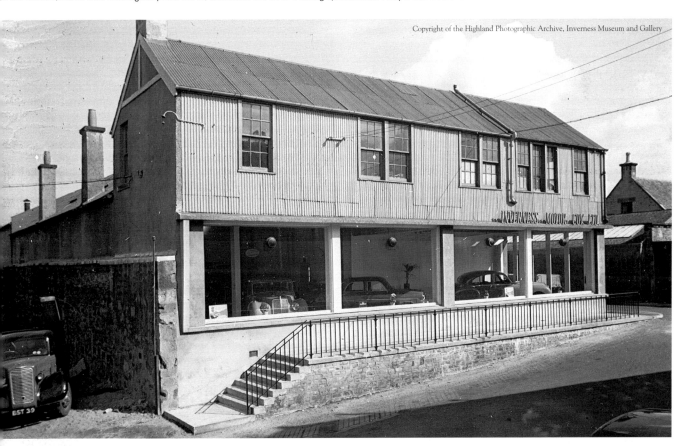

INVERNESS MOTOR COMPANY SHOWROOM

This photo taken by the late Jimmy Nairn in the 1950s, shows Inverness Motor Company's showroom on the corner of Strothers Lane and Railway Terrace, on the site now occupied by the Post Office sorting office. The British-built cars in the window are from left, an Armstrong Siddeley Sapphire, a Ford Zephyr Mk I and a Jaguar Mk VII. The elderly tipper lorry registered BST39, beside the showroom, is a Rootes Group-built Commer dating from around 1945.

OLD ACADEMY

This was the original Inverness Royal Academy building, which gave Academy Street its name. The Old Royal Academy building was erected in 1792, to take over pupils and some of the staff of the town's Grammar School, situated since 1668 on the site of the present Dunbar Centre. The building in this photo was used as a school until 1895 when the Academy moved to Midmills Road. The Academy left that building in 1979, for a new site at Culduthel. This building, despite several redevelopment threats, still exists, albeit in much altered form, with the ground floor taken up by a pub and shops.

OLD STONE BRIDGE

This is a print of the old Stone Bridge in Inverness, sketched some time between 1836, when the southern wing of the present Inverness Castle was built, and 1848, when the northern wing was added for use as a jail. Built in 1685, the Stone Bridge had seven arches and was said to have been partly built of stone from a demolished fort erected by Oliver Cromwell when his soldiers were based in Inverness. In the bridge's third pier, a vault was built to be used as a prison, measuring only six feet in height and covering an area of ten feet by seven feet. The Stone bridge was carried away by the great flood of 1849. In the middle of the picture, women can be seen washing laundry in the River Ness.

BUILDINGS AND VIEWS YOU MAY RECOGNISE

RAINING'S STAIRS

Raining's Stairs, the steep passage linking Ardconnel Street with Castle Street, commemorates a Norwich merchant, John Raining, who in 1726 bequeathed £1,200 to establish a fund supporting charitable schools in the Highlands. The trust was administered by The Society for the Propagation of Christian Knowledge which built a three-storey school at the end of Ardconnel Street in 1757. Extensions were added in 1840 and 1881, but by 1894 the pupils had been transferred to the nearby High School in what is now Crown Primary School. The building was demolished in 1976. Most of the buildings lining the stairs have also long gone, or have been replaced, but the Town House, seen in this 20th Century photo, on the other side of Castle Street, remains very much the same.

ROSE ST, INNES ST, LONGMAN ROAD JUNCTION 1950s

In the 1950s this was the rather untidy junction of Innes Street, Rose Street, Longman Road and Railway Terrace, looking west towards Academy Street and the spire of the Old High Church. This area of Inverness has been completely restructured in recent years, with much of the area to the left now the site of the very ugly, but functional Rose Street Car Park. The attractive black car approaching is a Rootes Group Humber Hawk Mk V or VI, then very popular with the affluent middle classes. The Coventry-based Rootes Brothers, Lord William and Sir Reginald, both owned small estates in Sutherland, where they and their employees frequently tested the prototypes of new models. The family sold the group to Chrysler in 1967, and it faded out in 1978. The lorry behind the Humber is a wartime utility Bedford of a pattern made for the armed forces.

Copyright of the Highland Photographic Archive, Inverness Museum and Gallery

STREET URCHINS IN WATERLOO PLACE

Although all of these street urchins caught in time sitting at the corner of Portland Place and Waterloo Place are barefooted, it is interesting to note that most, like their modern counterparts are following the fashion of the day, in this case by wearing flat caps. The shop sign on Waterloo Place is for Waterloo Cash Grocery, Tea, Wine and Spirit Merchant.

CASTLE STREET DEMOLITIONS 1967

The northern side of Castle Street, running along the bottom of a rather unstable Castle Hill, suffered a number of landslips in the 20th Century, the most notable almost certainly being that of October 1932, when several homes were destroyed, fortunately without loss of life, and the families occupying them had to be evacuated.

The remaining houses on that side of the street, between the Town House and the entrance to View Place, were finally demolished prior to a stabilisation and road widening scheme of 1967, which although it provided an attractive sloping garden beside the Castle, together with a car park extension, also, unfortunately, removed the quaint Victorian gothic gatehouse at its entrance.

ASTLE STREET DEMOLITIONS 1967

is photo shows the final stages of the Castle Street demolitions in 1967, prior to the creation of a sloping garden, road widening and car park extension.

WAVERLEY HOTEL FIRE 1940s

This photo of the aftermath of a disastrous fire which swept through the Waverley Hotel in Union Street, Inverness, during the war, was taken by a passer-by from Lombard Street. Note the covered nearside headlamp on the pre-war Austin saloon in the foreground, registered KG 8188, a sure indication of the "black-out" which prevailed during hostilities. Also, the sign on the Farm Produce Store at the left proclaims: "We are blackened out, but you are not shut out. Come in." Is the young lass running up the street still in town?

INVERNESS CASTLE 1930s

Inverness Castle, dating from around the mid-1930s, with some old cannon and a German field howitzer, captured at Loos by the Queen's Own Cameron Highlanders 1915, still outside the front door. It was later moved to the entrance hall inside the main front door of the castle. Local Highland councillor Donnie Kerr, who has been seek information about the weapon, has traced it to the Clan Cameron Museum at Achnacarry Castle, Lochaber, where clan chief and Inverness-shire county councillor Colo Sir Donald Cameron, at some time in the 1960s, offered it a place of refuge when the authorities sought to dispose of it. Donnie, who has been told that the cannon are s in storage, would like to see them restored to a public place of prominence. The castle main door has long since been sealed up, and the former entrance hall and adjoin rooms long since converted to form Inverness Sheriff Court's Courtroom 2.

INVERNESS AERIAL 1963

This photo was taken around the end of 1963 or ea the following year, shortly after the south end of Bri Street was demolished to make way for the prese box-like structure. Move along Church Street from t Town Steeple and you can still see on the east side of t street the popular Northern Meeting Rooms, which ea weekend hosted two dances at a time, and on its west s the equally-loved Old Caledonian Hotel. Both fell vic shortly afterwards to the lemming rush for new gerryb developments inspired by a perceived increase in ratea values.

INVERNESS AERIAL – TRAIN STATION

When this photo was taken, Inverness Railway Station was a much more significant site than it is today. The magnificent round engine house was still standing, but with diesel engines already predominating, it was due for a quick dispatch. Note the huge numbers of freight wagons, now, sadly, a rarity on Highland railways, as modern commerce seems to prefer the huge pantechnicons which congest today's A9 trunk road and other seminal arteries to and from the north.

CATHEDRAL HORSE CARVING

This small carving, high on one of Inverness Cathedral's grand windows offers us a bit of a mystery. The popular theory is that it is a memorial to a horse which was killed whe
a pulley rope broke and a block of stone fell on it during construction of the building from 1866, when the foundation stone was laid, and completion in 1869. It is said the hors
was the only casualty during those three years and that the workmen were so upset by the death that they decided to leave a lasting memorial. Recently, however, an alternati
story has come to light from an American who said he was the great grandson of stonemason David Allison who had worked on the historic building. He advised that his gre
grandfather, who liked a dram, would get into his cart after "a few too many" at his local and tell the horse to take him home. The horse always got him there safely – but n
before taking a detour and stopping at the stonemason's grandfather's home in Carlton Terrace, off Millburn Road, to get an apple from his grandmother. Mr Allison was s
attached to the animal that he created the carving while completing work on the cathedral, the story goes.

RAIGMORE FILLING STATION 1970

Although this picture of Raigmore Filling Station and Caravan Park was only taken in 1970, the Safeway complex which replaced it soon afterwards has long since been deserted, and is at time of publication being demolished to make way for another retail development. Note in the distance the Longman fields, with cattle still grazing where industrial and commercial buildings now stand, and also smoke from fires at the municipal dump – no hint of greenhouse gases and sustainable eco-systems in those not-so-faraway days.

INVERNESS AERIAL

This picture, looking south, shows clearly in the lower centre, the dome of what is now called the Victorian Market, and immediately above it the ruin of the Methodist Chapel, gutted by fire in the early 1960s.

INVERNESS AERIAL – MILBURN ACADEMY

Note in the centre of this aerial view the then recent completed first phase of Millburn Academy, with cricket match in progress in its grounds. In 2008 th building, which experienced quality and maintenanc problems throughout its relatively short life, we demolished following the construction of a new scho on the playing fields.

RAILWAY TERRACE COTTAGES 1988

This row of cottages in Railway Terrace was already boarded up and awaiting demolition when this photo was taken in 1988.

Faces, Not Places

BALLOCH SCHOOL P7 1986
This photo of Primary 7 pupils from Balloch Primary was taken for the Highland News by well-known local photographer the late Norrie MacLeod, in June 1986, as they were about to embark on a trip to Edinburgh, shortly before leaving that school for the last time.

PLAYGROUP 1978
The pre-school playgroup held at St Stephen's Church Hall, pictured at their Christmas party in December 1978. Now in their mid-30s, they're scattered far afield, with at least one, Mark Cruden, sixth from left, rear row, in New Zealand.

CENTRAL SCHOOL PRIMARY 7 1964

The children pictured here were soon to embark on the great adventure of promotion to secondary school, when they assembled in 1964, during their last days in Primary 7 at Central School.

CENTRAL PRIMARY SCHOOL CLASS 1933

This photo of a class at Central Primary School in 1933 was sent in by Betty Mackay, of Bellfield Park, whose cousin Donald Mackay is the fair-haired boy second from the left in the front row. The class was probably Primary 4, as Donald was eight at the time. In adult life he became a senior cameraman with the BBC in Manchester, but his ashes were interred at Tore Cemetery, in the Black Isle, following his death in 2005, aged 80. Mrs Mackay wonders how many survivors of this class remain, and whether they could identify other children in the photograph.

The Piper Recalls

Invernessian John M Allan ended a distinguished 35-year army career as director of the Army School of Piping at Edinburgh Castle, retiring in 1990, after nine years in this prestigious post, as a major with an MBE in recognition of his services.

After serving his time as a plumber with local firm A J Russell & Sons, he was called up for National Service in 1956, and decided to sign on as a regular piper with the Scots Guards, having learned to play the pipes from his father John C Allan and in the Boys' Brigade. His progress was swift, and having passed his pipe-major's course within three years of enlisting, he transferred in 1962 to the Queen's Own Highlanders as pipe-major, being appointed pipe-major instructor at the Army School of Piping two years later. Commissioned in 1979, he became piping school director in 1981, the third officer ever to be appointed to the Army's top piping post.

John and his wife Jean, who now live in Penicuik, but who visit Croy regularly, sent us many interesting pictures depicting life in the Inverness of half a century ago, some of which we feature in the following five pages.

7TH BB COY PT TEAM 1949
The fit youngsters in this group were members of 7th Inverness Company Boys' Brigade physical training team in 1949. Standing, from left, are: Jimmy Nairne, Alex Chisholm, Stanley Bartlett, John Allan, Bobby MacKenzie, Billy Panton and Angie MacPhee. Seated, from left, are: Sylvia Cameron, company pianist, Dave Petrie, Charlie MacKenzie and John MacKenzie (captain).

BOYS' BRIGADE PIPE BAND MEMBERS, CARRBRIDGE, 1949
Carrbridge Station was the scene of this happy snap of Inverness Boys' Brigade Pipe Band members arriving in the village for summer camp in 1949. Standing, from left are:
Finlay MacKenzie, Jock Skinner, Kellas Cameron, John Smith, Jim Wardrop, Ian MacLeod; kneeling: John Allan, Tommy Cameron, Tom Wilson.

MERKINCH SCHOOL, MR FRASER'S CLASS 1948
This group, so typical of a school photo of long ago, was Mr Fraser's class at Merkinch School, in 1948.

7TH (QUEEN STREET CHURCH) COY BOYS' BRIGADE, 1949
The whole of 7th (Queen Street Church) Company Boys' Brigade, mustered in front of Central School for this photo in 1949. The senior members, seated in front, from left, are: Alex MacAskill, Evan Lumsden, Henry Bissett, Danny Craig, John Mackenzie (captain), Alex Shand, Dave Petrie, Tommy Cameron, Donnie MacAskill and Jackie Panton. John Allan, who passed this photo on, is standing second from right. Evan Lumsden, then a detective sergeant, and a colleague Constable Ian Ritchie, died tragically, but heroically, 40 years ago, as they dived in the Caledonian Canal at Corpach in an attempt to rescue a missing member of the public.

INVERNESS BRITISH LEGION PIPE BAND AT MAYFIELD HOME 1951
Members of Inverness British Legion Pipe Band are pictured here around 1951, along with Highland dancers, after entertaining residents at Mayfield Home of Rest. The drum major was Dennis Curran and the pipe major Donald MacRae. The big drummer, centre, rear, wearing leopard skin, was Sandy Macpherson, who also had his own dance band.

INVERNESS P&D MEMBERS, BERLIN 1967
These Inverness members of the Pipes and Drums of 1st Battalion Queen's Own Highlanders, were pictured outside Wavell Barracks, Berlin, in 1967, preparing for a formal event. From left are: Lance-Corporal Kenny Griffin, Lance-Corporal Jackie Urquhart, Piper John Simpson, who also danced and Pipe-Major John M Allan.

INVERNESS PIPING SOCIETY'S EARLY MEETING
This historic photo of the newly-formed Inverness Piping Society was snapped in the Curling Club's hut at Culcabock Road, Inverness, in 1947, shortly after the society's formation. Note the number of uniformed members from Fort George, the Cameron Barracks or the local Territorials. The war was less than three years over, the Malayan Emergency was just starting, while the Korean War and Kenyan Emergency were still in the future. Playing to an enthusiastic, but no doubt critical audience, is Pipe-Major Evan Macrae, of the Queen's Own Cameron Highlanders, while listening raptly, from left, are: Unidentified; Jackie Chisholm; John Allan; Pipe-Major Stewart MacNaughton, Cameron Highlanders; Sergeant Robert "Mickey" Mackay, Camerons; Pipe-Major Donald MacLeod, Seaforth Highlanders; Norman Macrae; Dr Robert Simpson; Sheriff John P Grant of Rothiemurchus; Archie MacRae; John MacKenzie and Pipe-Major Donald MacDonald, Army Cadet Force,

BOYS' BRIGADE BAND 1947
Marching to the War Memorial on Remembrance Day 1947 are these members of Inverness Boys' Brigade Pipe Band. Those in the front row, from left, are: John Hunter, Tommy Cameron, John Allan and Kellas Cameron.

INVERNESS CRICKET CLUB 1927
These members of Inverness Cricket Club were snapped in the Northern Meeting Park in 1927, along with, left, Pipe Major Robert Meldrum (1851-1935) and Piper John C Allan (1903-72), father and initial teacher of Major John M Allan, who became director of the Army School of Piping at Edinburgh Castle.

A J RUSSELL & SONS (PLUMBERS) STAFF SOCIAL 1953

Invernessians and others from across the Highlands remember with pleasure and nostalgia Burnett's Tearooms in Academy Street, the venue for this staff social, in December 1953, of A J Russell & Sons, Plumbers. The young man in the centre, with his arms folded, is the boss, Donald Davidson, who kept the original name when he bought the business over. John Allan, who gave us the photo, is the young apprentice on the left of the front row.

MASSED BANDS REHEARSING AT CAMERON BARRACKS, AUG 1964

This historic picture, taken at the Cameron Barracks in August 1964, shows the massed bands of the 1st Battalion Queen's Own Highlanders, 4th/5th Battalion Queen's Own Cameron Highlanders and 11th Battalion Seaforth Highlanders rehearsing prior to beating retreat in the burgh's Union Street. The meeting of the three bands was unusual, perhaps even unique, as the regular army battalions of the Seaforths and Camerons had amalgamated in 1961 to form the Queen's Own Highlanders. The TA Seaforth and Cameron battalions soldiered on, with their headquarters at Dingwall and the Cameron Barracks repectively, until the end of March 1967, when the Ministry of Defence did what neither Napoleon, the Kaiser, nor Hitler was able to do, and consigned them to the dustbin of obscurity. The Queen's Own later amalgamated with the Gordon Highlanders to form The Highlanders, but even this battalion has now been absorbed into the amorphous Royal Regiment of Scotland, as its 4th Battalion. The distinguished front rank in the photo, shows, from left: Pipe Maj John M Allan, QOHldrs; Cpl Andy Venters, QOHldrs; Pipe Maj John Burgess, 4/5 Camerons; Drum Maj Jimmy Watson, 11 Seaforths; Sgt Tommy Urquhart, 4/5 Camerons; unidentified; Pipe Maj John Riach, 11 Seaforths.

ST JOSEPH'S RC SCHOOL
The scene here is St Joseph's RC School around 1946. Although the war had recently been won, Britain remained in the grip of grave austerity, but these pupils were still smiling. They are from left: Dennis Hill, Leslie Johnstone, Donnie MacKenzie, Norman MacLeod, Francis Thorne, Peter Baird, Robert Shields, Ronnie Ross, Tony O'Connor, Ward Gilchrist, Hamish Paterson, Jack Ross, Ronnie Tulloch, Andrew Cameron, Jamie Carrol and Stewart MacLennan, who sent in this photograph.

AUCTION TIME
This photograph shows buyers and sellers attending a cattle auction at Inverness Mart about 1955.

CHILDREN ON CUMBERLAND STONE

The children sitting on the Cumberland Stone at Culloden Moor are thought to have been taking part in a Sunday School outing. The stone lies east of the Keppoch Inn, east of the battlefield, and is an enormous glacial boulder associated with the Duke of Cumberland. According to local lore, the "Butcher" directed the Government forces at the Battle of Culloden (1746) from the top of the boulder, but this claim seems fanciful, as contemporary records state that he was on horseback between his first and second lines during the action. However, he may well at some point have stood on it, as it has been there since the end of the last Ice Age.

TOYLAND

World War II was little over a year old when these children of the Convent School at Huntley Lodge, Southside Road, spread a little merriment at one of the gloomiest periods in Britain's history, by taking part in this show, Toyland at Christmas Time, in 1940. Rear row, from left: Felicity Bruce-Watt, Simon Gossip, Morag Davie, unidentified, Therese MacRae, Sonia Morris, Rhona Gilchrist; middle row, from left: Peter Chisholm, Raymond Morris, E Macpherson, Elma Davie, "Twinka" Morrison, Robin -, Pat Magee, Pamela Davie; front from left; Mario Celli, Leonella Ferrari, Ivor Morris, Kenneth Morris, unidentified, Renato Ferrari, unidentified, unidentified.

MACKINTOSH FAMILY

K J Mackintosh was a well-known and respected business in the Eastgate, selling prams, radios, television sets and record players. It was forced to move to Baron Taylor's Lane when the Eastgate was largely demolished to make way for Marks & Spencer and the adjoining shopping centre. Pictured here, with their mother, in the 1950s, obviously about to depart for a formal event, are the late Gordon Mackintosh (left) and his brother Dennis, who between them ran the shop.

GORDON'S GARAGE

The range of services offered by Gordon's Garage in the 1950s is well advertised here. The people in the photo are, from left: Flora Gordon, Margaret Fraser, Cheryl Gordon, Danny Ross and Phyllis Gordon.

JIMMY NAIRN AT WORK 1980

After the Playhouse Cinema burned down in 1972, Jimmy Nairn continued to recreate his annual Christmas Disney Wonderworld on a smaller scale in his own home, fo children of friends and neighbours. Here he's showing one of his puppets to 19-months old Simeon Graf, while the wee boy's mother Romola looks on happily. Romola' brother Ron Miller, a talented amateur cine-cameraman and photographer, learned the cine-photography craft from Jimmy, and repaid his mentor by making a short film about his achievements. Simeon is now a graduate electrical engineer.

JIMMY NAIRN AND SIMEON

Jimmy Nairn shows a mechanical toy to little Simeon Graf.

RON MILLER 1970s
Inverness-born optician and talented amateur cine-photographer, the late Ron Miller, made many short films, now fortunately safe in the national archives. Ron died in 1991, aged 57.

RON MILLER MAKING FILM
The scene is the lounge of retired Playhouse Cinema manager Jimmy Nairn's house shortly before Christmas 1976. Jimmy Nairn, an ardent cine-photographer from early days, thought to have made Scotland's first ever "talkie" home movie. Even after the Playhouse burned down in 1972, the marvellously resourceful Jimmy used to decorate his own home specially for Christmas and invite local children in to enjoy on a smaller scale the marvels of Disneyland he used to create each year in the Playhouse café, before disaster struck. The man filming the occasion is Jimmy's friend and fellow cine-enthusiast, the late Ron Miller. Ron, an optician by profession, but a cine-photographer by inclination, made many excellent short films, including one about Jimmy's life and work.

JOHN GRANT 1980

John Grant from Edinburgh, creator of the well-known children's caveboy cartoon character Littlenose, is here entertaining children at a 1980 meeting of Inverness Children's Book Group in the Spectrum Centre. John Grant originally invented Littlenose to entertain his own children, but it went on to become a global success, both on television and in book form. He wrote and illustrated at least 13 Littlenose books between 1968 and 1993.

APPLECROSS SEARCH

There was no such requirement as a risk assessment, nor were tight health and safety regulations to the fore, when Inverness firemen Willie Shand and his colleague Gordon Taylor, both very experienced swimmers, who had been experimenting unofficially with new underwater breathing equipment, were asked by the late Ross-shire councillor George Cumming to search a river pool near Applecross for a missing schoolteacher in March 1959. Note the rather basic safety precautions, of ropes. It was bitterly cold recalls Willie, now 84, but copious drams of malt whisky administered during the search, helped to keep the chill at bay. What would today's administrators of "'elf'n safety" have made of the operation? It's more likely that Willie, pictured nearest the camera, and Gordon would have been carpeted rather than commended for their courage and public-spiritedness. Sadly, they didn't find the lady, whose body was discovered a month later, on a lonely moor.

APPLECROSS SEARCH (see opposite page also)
Willie and Gordon (right) are pictured here swathed in blankets after taking part in the search. Willie recalls that colleagues accompanying them made cracks about "yetis", on seeing them clad like this. Gordon, who died some years ago, was known as "The Baron", and was also a very good singer.

SENIOR OFFICERS, NORTHERN AREA FIRE BRIGADE 1966
These were the senior officers of Northern Area Fire Service in 1966 shortly after its transfer to its new headquarters in Harbour Road, Inverness. From left are: John Howie, Willie Shand, Deputy Firemaster Harper, Firemaster Eric McIntyre, Ian Chisholm, Lyall McRobb.

NORTHERN AREA FIRE BRIGADE 1952

In 1941 Inverness Town Council Fire Brigade was absorbed into the wartime National Fire Service, organised into 11 regions, Scotland being the eleventh. After the war, the Government introduced the Fire Services Act in 1947, to transfer firefighting functions throughout Britain from the National Fire Service to fire brigades maintained by groups of local authorities. The newly-created Northern Area Fire Brigade covered the counties of Caithness, Sutherland, Ross & Cromarty, Inverness, Orkney, Shetland and Inverness burgh. In 1975, when local government was reorganised, the brigade was renamed the Northern Fire Brigade, while again, in February 1983, the name changed to Highland and Islands Fire Brigade. These Inverness firemen were pictured outside the Northern Area Fire Brigade headquarters then based at the town's Fraser Park, from which the service flitted to its current base in Harbour Road the following decade. It has recently undergone another name change to H&I Fire and Rescue.

PIPERS' RALLY

This is not an opening scene from the World Pipe Band Championships of 1966, as we thought at first, when we received it from Highland dancing enthusiast Olive Gunn in a box of slides taken by her late husband James, from Kiltarlity, a former soldier and a keen pipe band fan. The pipers marched from the burgh centre, seen here as it was around 1959, to the Bught Park, with lots of spectators watching them enthusiastically every step of the way. Among interesting old buildings, from left, are a corner of the Bank of Scotland, the former Woolworth's Store, replaced some years later by a modern building, following a fire, the gothic Highland Club building, still in existence as a hostel, and the Northern Hotel, demolished in the 1970s to make way for a new shops and office block.

VE DAY PARTY 1945
Despite shortages and privations caused by nearly six years of war, residents in Columba Road and Caledonian Road celebrated Victory in Europe Day on May 8, 1945, by holding a huge party at Central School. Do any of the tiny tots in this photo recognise themselves?

SUNDAY AT THE BUGHT PARK 1954
Best suits or sports jackets, in most cases with collars and ties, were the accepted uniform for teenage boys walking out on a Sunday in the mid-20th Century, as this photo taken at the Bught Park in 1954 demonstrates. The lads in the back row are: David Wallace, Donald Groat, Bill Robertson, Brian Main, Alf MacDonald; front: A McInnes, S "Poker" MacLennan, B Fraser, Ally Chisholm and B "Grannie" Grant.

GOLDEN WEDDING CELEBRATIONS DAN AND GRACE FALCONER 1953
Dan Falconer was a well-known figure in the Merkinch area in the 1940s and '50s, where he was known as "The Tattie Man". He earned this nickname from his regular round with his horse and cart, selling vegetables. Here, he and his wife Grace, are pictured in the late 1960s, being congratulated on their diamond wedding anniversary by Provost William J Smith.

MUMS AND KIDS OF DRAKIES CUL-DE-SAC CELEBRATE THE ROYAL WEDDING IN 1981

The sorrows of a failed marriage for the late Princess Diana and Prince Charles were well in the future in 1981, when mums and children in Drakies Avenue cul-de-sac joined forces to celebrate what seemed then to be a fairytale wedding.

PET PARADE 1980s

We have no record of the winner of this pet parade, held at Drakies Avenue in the 1980s, but the judge was vet Jim Young, the tall man with his arms folded.

CHARLIE MACDONALD APRIL 1944
The scene is wartime Lindsay Avenue, Inverness, in April 1944, as smiling 19-year old Gunner Charlie MacDonald, then serving in a heavy anti-aircraft unit of the Royal Artillery, hugs the beloved family dog Cora, after returning home for a surprise leave.

5TH COMPANY BOYS' BRIGADE CIRCA 1948
The Boys' Brigade was popular in the burgh from its early days, and grew rapidly in influence in the first half of last century, with great sporting rivalry between the many companies which made up Inverness Battalion. This picture is of the 5th East Church Company, whose happy members have obviously won some trophy, although we have no details of what it was for. The young officer holding it, however, was Lamont Graham, who in working life was for many years manager of a wine shop in Queensgate. Was it the sheer ecstasy of the win that caused him to close his eyes, or did photographer Sandy McLaren, of Star Photos, have too bright a flash?

FAMILY GROUP 1973

The location where this charming little trio was pictured in March 1973 is not mentioned, but the driver of the wee car is Carolyn Shepherd, while the boy in the cowboy outfit is Robert MacBean, and the toddler standing up – presumably his sister – Alison MacBean.

FAMILY GROUP, KESSOCK STREET

The clothes these children are wearing, especially the garb of the little boy whose short trousers are held up with braces, suggest that the photo was taken well over 50 years ago. The location was the old air-raid shelter at 59 Kessock Street, and the youngsters are named as Christina, Art, Sally and Andrew Wood.

HIGHLAND OMNIBUSES STAFF 1950s

Lined up at the back of a Duple-built Bedford OB 29-seater bus, in the late 1950s, were these members of Highland Omnibuses' squad based at the Carse. In the pictur
are back row, left to right: Eddie Paterson, foreman, Isobel -, cleaner, Mrs Gilmoor, cleaner, Willie Brough, mechanic, Jess Ferguson, cleaner, Willie Junor, storeman, Charli
MacDonald, mechanic, - Harper, tyre fitter, Bob -, tyre fitter. Front row, left to right: - Forsyth, greaser, John Hawkins, mechanic, unknown, apprentice, Alistair Kid
shunter, unknown, tyre fitter.

INVERNESS BURGH POLICE 1949

When this photo of Inverness Burgh Police force was taken on 11th May, 1949, the chief constable, in the front row, middle, was Andrew Meldrum. Seated in front, on eithe
side, were the force's first two policewomen, Mona Urquhart on the left, and Betty Davis on the right. In those days of rather less than equal opportunity for women, Mon
had to resign her full-time job the following year on her marriage to colleague Dan Mackenzie (third from left, centre row), although the force was happy enough to retai
her services as an unpaid special constable. The little lady on the far left of the centre row is described as "Turnkey" Mrs Macdougall, a very old-fashioned name for jaile
Presumably her job was to lock up petty miscreants remanded in the police cells before their subsequent appearance at either the burgh police court or the sheriff court.

INVERNESS BURGH POLICE 1968

Inverness Burgh Police force had expanded slightly, and had moved from its Castle Wynd headquarters to the former Farraline Park School by the time this photograph was taken, prior to its amalgamation with Inverness-shire County Constabulary in November 1968, after a separate existence of 127 years. Chief constable at that time was Tom Sorley, seated, centre, with Sandy, the Highlands' first police dog at his feet. Immediately behind him is the north's first dog handler, Constable Dan Mackenzie, a well-kent figure nicknamed "Dan the Dog" as a result of his new vocation. Dan and Sandy, a powerful German shepherd, between them brought quite a few miscreants to justice before Sandy, like so many of his breed, fell victim to arthritis. It is of interest to note that the county force, founded on Hogmanay Day 1840, was responsible for policing in the town of Inverness from 1841 until 1847, when the burgh council decided it wanted its own force. Inverness-shire Constabulary was absorbed, along with other Highland and island police forces into Northern Constabulary in 1975.

LICENSED TRADE EVENT 1960s

There was reason to smile during this visit by Inverness licensees to Dewar's of Perth distillery around 40 years ago, as everyone seems to be clutching a presentation bottle of the golden liquid. Those of a certain age in the city will recognise many of these faces, such as Robbie Grigor, David Irvine, Bert Ross, Henry Munro, Angus MacLeod, Ernest Thomson, Walter Mackinnon and Willie MacGregor, whose daughter Rosemary sent this photo in.

TWO LITTLE GIRLS – INVERNESS 1949
These two little 10-year olds saunter happily arm in arm along Inverness High Street in 1949, quite unconcerned as traffic thunders by. The lass on the right is Olive Fraser and her wee chum is Patricia Paterson.

WAYFARERS TAKE A BREAK, CIRCA 1950
These lads of 5th (East Church) Company, Boys' Brigade were snapped taking a well-deserved break near Daviot on a trek to gain their wayfarers' badges.

ALICE BREWERY

Big Al makes his first delivery for the newly launched Alice Brewery in June, 1983. The brewery, producing a number of beers, including Alice Ale and Longman Lager, ran up until early 1988. Launched by Ollie Griffin and three other directors, it was called after Ollie's daughter and run from premises in Harbour Road. Pictured are well known Inverness blacksmith Simon MacDonald at Big Al's head, with the late Kenny Ross at the reigns and Candy Cameron of Dores sitting beside him. Also pictured are Citadel Bar owners, Bobby Clyne and his wife.

PUPPY LOVE

These collie pups were proving quite a handful for the Hendy sisters and their brother, photographed at Nuide Farm near Kingussie in 1936. Pictured left to right are Alma, Betty, Alastair and Nancy.

D CAMERON & CO

Not much in the way of time off to prepare for "the bells" a few decades ago. Staff and D Cameron & Co's shop at 21 Queensgate take a five minute break for the camera during stocktaking on Hogmanay 1965. Pictured are, left to right, Mr Graham, the manager, Eileen, Willie, Alma, Kathleen, Frances, Bruce, Eleanor, Rena and Neil.

MONKEY BUSINESS

Mr James Hendry makes friends with a rather unusual "family" which had been taken to the Black Isle Show as an attraction in 1974 or 1975. Some may recall one of the little fellas used to have a tipple from the top of a whisky bottle to entertain the crowds.

SHOEING TIME
Brothers Houstie, Sime and Charlie MacDonald with Willie Kennedy and Jock the horse at Inshes Smiddy in the 1950s. Jock beloned to Mr D MacKenzie at No 3 Inshes Holdings.

FRASER, KENNEDY AND FRASER
n Kennedy pictured in his shop In December 1972. The following August, Messrs W, I and J Kennedy announced they were retiring from business and thanked their many stomers for their support during many years of trading.

DRAKIES FARM
The site of Culcabock Golf Course with Drakies Farm in the background. The picture was taken in the late 1950s and shows pals Bill, Shortie, (back row) Houstie, J Duncan, Ben Duncan, B Cassie (middle row) Charlie, R Henry and Sime with dog Fruchie.

A TRIP ROUND THE PRINTERS
Smiling for the camera, pupils of Crown Primary school visit Highland Printers in March, 1980.

NVERNESS GIRLS' PIPE BAND, LATE 1940s

his photo of the first Inverness Girls' Pipe Band was taken in the late 1940s. Back row, from left: Vera Chambers, unidentified, Norah Macpherson, Myra Hunter; middle w, from left: unidentified, Sheila Reid, Roddy Ross (instructor), Sheila Mackintosh, Dave Ross (instructor), - Sutherland, unidentified; front, from left: Jessie Cumming, nidentified.

ISHOP EDEN'S SCHOOL 1947

his class, so typical of its time, was snapped with teacher, Mrs Cattanach, outside Bishop Eden's School, in 1947. Rear, from left: unidentified, John King, Leslie Mackay, om Fraser, Novello Macdonald, unidentified, James Melville; third row, from left: Derick McCalman, Charlie Cameron, Elizabeth Cameron, Babs Anderson, Rosemary alconer, Audrey Johnstone, Donalda Williams, Evelyn Graham, Maureen Mackenzie, unidentified, Peter Kay; second row, from left: Isabel Ross, Marsaili, Mackenzie, lildred Macrae, Grace Hepburn, Margaret Mackenzie, Mona Ross, Peggy Crout, Maris Watt, Audrey Johnstone, Laura Lobban; front: unidentified, unidentified unidentified, mes Johnstone.

NURSES' CONCERT
This appears to have been one of the annual Christmas carol concerts held by Inverness nurses in aid of local charities.

NURSES RNI 1952
This group of young nurses was pictured at the Royal Northern Infirmary in 1952.

HEILAN' MAN

H. MacDonald, heavily disguised as a wild Highlander, took first prize and was awarded a cup in a fancy dress competition at Viewhill Gymkhana in Autust 1982. But she couldn't have done it without the help of Cinders – who also got into the spirit of the occasion and was dressed up in great detail also, right down to his tartan and heather-stuffed puttees.

CROWN PRIMARY SCHOOL CLASS 2A 1960-61

Crown Primary School Class 2A 1960-61. Rear from left: Ronald Stewart, John Beaton, Ian Rhodes, unidentified, Ian Macpherson, Victor Fornari, Ian Black, Jan Milne, Robert Bruce, Alastair Fraser; third row, from left; Derek Munro, Colin Mackenzie, Rory Matheson, Graham Quinney, David Davidson, Raymond Tulloch, Gordon Cripps, Neil Glass, Alastair Williams; second row, from left: Valerie Fraser, unidentified, Avril McIntosh, Judith Duncan, Grace Rennie, Wilma Mackie, unidentified, Margaret Macfarlane, Morven Chisholm, unidentified; front, from left: Lesley Lawson, unidentified, Rhona Annand, Linda Currie, Amanda Wotherspoon, Judith Noble, Joanna Campbell, Sheila Critchley, unidentified, Evelyn Rae, Mary Blaikie, Patricia Cobham.

CROWN PRIMARY SCHOOL CLASS 2B 1961-62

Crown Primary School Class 2B 1961-62. Rear from left: Lawrence -, Sandy Macdonald, Hugh Jack, Douglas MacInnes, Hugh Merrilees, William Williams, Ken MacLean, Adrian Gavin; third row, from left: Stewart -, George Geddes, unidentified, Alastair Batchen, Hamish -, Alastair Orrock, Derek Morton, unidentified, Jimmy Boggon, John Johnston; second row, from left: Janice Tawse, Elma McRitchie, Sheena Macdonald, Theresa Seddon, Morag Moore, Judith Ferguson, Wilma Mackie, Anne Sutherland, Rosemary Calder, Fiona McIntosh; front from left: Laura Scott, Lorraine -, Anne Cleeton, Anne Munro, Audrey Sime, Eileen -, Joyce -, Iris Spence, Josephine Gunn, Gabrielle Barking, Christine Chrystall, Deirdre MacKenzie.

CENTRAL PRIMARY SCHOOL

Pupils of Primary 7 at Central Primary, pictured in 1973.

HIGH SCHOOL DAYS
A group of third year pupils from their days at Inverness High School around 1969 – class 2B or 3B.

POLICE BALL
Officers, partners and friends of Inverness Burgh Police force at their dinner dance pictured in the mid 1960s.

COUNCIL WORKMATES

Staff of the registrar's, housing and social work departments based at the Parish Council Building in Bank Street pictured in March 1968. Centre front is George MacBean, Registrar at the time.

CO-OP STAFF

A very early picture of the Inverness Co-operative Society building in Church Street when it had a dedicated bakery section.

IVERNESS HIGH SCHOOL CLASS VI 1959
bout to face the world of tertiary education or the start of their careers were these Class VI pupils of Inverness High School in 1959.

ENTRAL SCHOOL PRIMARY 7 1953
hortly to leave junior school for the trauma of secondary education were these Primary 7 pupils of Central School, pictured in 1953.

ORTHOPAEDIC DEPARTMENT DANCE EARLY 1960s
Members of staff of Raigmore Hospital's Orthopaedic department are here pictured enjoying their staff dance at the Cummings Hotel in the early 1960s.

HIGHLAND COLLEGE OF NURSING
Registered, psychiatric and enrolled nurses with their certificates from Highland College of Nursing after successfully passing their final exams.

NATIVITY SCENE
These youngsters were pictured taking part in a Nativity play at Leachkin School in the 1950s.

SCOTTISH BAKERS' UNION INVERNESS ANNUAL BUS TRIP
Members of Inverness branch of the Scottish Bakers' Union and family members pause briefly for a photograph before setting off for their annual bus run in a double-decker, well over 60 years ago. The man at the rear, left, is George Ralph, at that time branch secretary and employed at the NAAFI in Diriebught Road, while beside him, with his arm around his son is NAAFI foreman Dick Macrae. The dark-haired lady second from right is Dick's wife, and the lass on the left is Louise Taylor, still, after many years, a popular star of Inverness Opera Company. Louise can't remember why she was on the trip, but thinks it may have been because her mother worked part-time in the NAAFI. Note the advert on the back of the bus for what was then probably the Highlands' most celebrated toyshop, Walker's Emporium, on the corner of Inglis Street and Baron Taylor's Street. It closed in 1958.

REDPATH-CHAMBERS WEDDING 1947

When Inverness girl Catherine Chambers married Angus Redpath from Lancaster in his home town, in the austerity days of December 1947, less than three years after World War II, the bride and her mother-in-law, Violet Redpath, made the wedding dress from surplus parachute silk, then a very desirable commodity. Her sister Vera Mackinnon who lives in Glendoe Terrace, recalls: "They were sitting up late the night before, sewing the buttons on, and worried that they weren't going to get it finished." Catherine who before her marriage worked in Young & Chapman's store in Union Street, met her husband, of Scottish origin, and then stationed with the Navy at Invergordon, when he came into the shop with a friend. The couple, who still live in Lancaster, celebrated their diamond anniversary last year, and have five of a family. They have 13 grandchildren and nine-great-grandchildren.

A SAGESSE CONVENT SCHOOL

pils of the La Sagesse convent school pictured around 70 years ago. There are a few names written on the back of the photo, indicating the presence of a Mackay, a King
d a Chisholm in the back row, and two Chisholms in the centre row. It's a little more specific about the front row, pointing out Mario Celli, fifth left; Twinka Morrison, sixth
t; Theresa Macrae, centre; Bianco Turriani fifth right; and Ian Macrae, sixth right.

NVERNESS TECHNICAL HIGH SCHOOL 1954/55

he boys of Mr Cummings class at Inverness Technical High School in 1954/55 are, back row, left to right: Donald MacAskill, unknown, unknown, Tommy Walker, George
acAskill, Ian Sutherland, Angus MacDonald, Brian Davidson. Middle row, left to right: Mr Cumming, David Gordon, Hector Munro, Mackenzie Rhind, David Mellis, unknown,
known, Ian Young, John MacPherson. Seated, left to right: Victor Armstrong, unknown, unknown, Gordon Leadingham, Jimmy Davidson, Brian White, Jimmy -, Angus
acDonald, Kerr MacKintosh. Front row, left to right: Harry Smith, Tommy Sutherland, Douglas Urquhart, Alisdair MacDonald, Francis MacWilliams, Andrew Smith and Eddie
x.

Changing Transport Needs

HMS BRITON

This former sailing frigate, launched in 1814, only nine years after the Battle of Trafalgar, was sent to the breaker's yard a century ago this year, having served for t
previous 32 years as the Royal Naval Reserve's training ship at Inverness. Originally named HMS Brilliant, she was the veteran of several naval engagements when stripp
of masts, roofed over and fitted out as a drill ship for the RNR in 1860. She was based at London, Aberdeen and Dundee before being towed in 1876 to Inverness, whe
in 1889 she was was renamed HMS Briton. The vessel was also used for a time as a floating barracks by the local militia. Her name lives on as the name of Inverness S
Cadets' headquarters at South Kessock.

Copyright of the Highland Photographic Archive, Inverness Museum and Gallery

CABMEN, MACRAE & DICK

The smart bowler-hatted men are cabmen employed around the end of the 19th Century by the burgeoning transport services concern Macrae & Dick. Their more casua
dressed colleagues are possibly ostlers and maintenance staff. In 1878, Roderick Macrae of Beauly and William Dick of Redcastle became business partners in a firm th
offered horses and horse-drawn carriages for hire and also acted as a posting agency. With the arrival of the motor car early the next century, Macrae & Dick becar
interested not only in the hiring of cars but also in the servicing and sale of vehicles. As this part of the business increased, the horse hiring and posting element decline
Today, the company, which moved to the Longman Industrial Estate from its town-centre bases at Academy Street and Strothers Lane, is still one of the leading mo
industry firms in the north of Scotland.

Copyright of the Highland Photographic Archive, Inverness Museum and Gallery

HIGHLAND GLAZING DELIVERY VAN

This photo from the David Whyte Studio archives shows a Bedford delivery lorry, registration UST 880, belonging to the Highland Glazing Co Ltd, taken in 1963 outside Inverness Fire Station. The firm which owned it was based at 32a Waterloo Place. In the background are an early 1950s Morris Oxford, left, and a contemporary Morris 1000.

Copyright of the Highland Photographic Archive, Inverness Museum and Gallery

INVERNESS RAILWAY STATION LATE VICTORIAN ERA

Inverness Station was designed by the Highland Railway engineer Joseph Mitchell. It opened for passenger services on 7 November 1855 and for freight trains on 3 December of the same year. From then on, the station played an increasingly important role in the expansion of the Highland Capital, both as a commercial centre and a tourist destination. The stationmaster in this Victorian picture is said to be a Mr Forbes.

JAGUAR IN INVERNESS MOTOR COMPANY SHOWROOM

The car in the foreground of Inverness Motor Company's showroom is a luxurious Jaguar Mk VII sports saloon, of which nearly 31,000 were produced in Britain between 195 and 1956. Immediately behind is a Ford Zephyr Mk I, the manufacturer's second top of the range British model, while beyond it is another limousine, an Armstrong Siddele Sapphire, another icon of bygone motoring days.

LORD LOVAT'S FIRST CAR

Driving along beside the River Nes is one of the earliest cars seen in th burgh. This 10-horsepower French-bu Panhard et Levassor was registered o ST 9 on 31 December 1903 by Simo Joseph Fraser (1871-1933), 14th Lor Lovat and 23rd chieftain of the Lova Frasers, of Beaufort Castle, Beaul While legally the 14th peer, as tw generations of his ancestors has bee divested of the title after the 174 rising, he liked to style himself the 16 Lord Lovat. In 1899 he raised the Lova Scouts for service in the Boer War, an also served in World War I, in whic he commanded the Highland Mounte Brigade as a brigadier-general. Lo Lovat was also first chairman of th Forestry Commission, from 1919 t 1927, and served in Stanley Baldwin Conservative Government from 192 27, as Under-Secretary of State fo Dominion Affairs. This desirab registration, used throughout h lifetime by his heir, war hero an commando leader, the 15th Lor Lovat, is still thought to belong to th Lovat family.

THREE OLD CARS

These three doctors' cars, lined up at South Kessock over a century ago, were among the first seen in Inverness. Pictured are Driver Cameron and Dr Nicholson, (ST7); Dr Brown (ST6); Driver Whyte and Dr George William England Kerr (ST8). According to the register of motor cars for Inverness, the cars were registered by Dr Kerr on 31 December 1903. ST 6 and 7 are Arrol-Johnstons of differing types, while ST8 is a Toledo steam car, 16 cwt.

VINTAGE CAR AT GORDON'S GARAGE

Cheryl Gordon, the owner's young daughter is the girl behind the wheel of this vintage motor, while on the right is her mother Phyllis, and on the other side mechanic, the late Kenny Malcolm. According to scant records available, the car, which looks almost pre-World War I, was in fact first registered with the number ST 2782 to Macrae & Dick on 4th April 1924. Kenny Malcolm, a popular figure in Inverness, and highly regarded in his trade, carved his own tiny niche in local history by being the first person in the town to be breathalysed after a dram too many.

The earliest buses to make an appearance during the Edwardian era in Inverness, as elsewhere, were almost certainly charabancs, from the French "char-a-banc" – open-topped vehicles with banks or rows of seats, often locally coach-built on lorry chassis, sometimes with hoods to keep out the worst of the rain, if not the wind. In its most refined form, the charabanc survived until well into the 1920s. The first bus registered in Inverness-shire in the early 20th Century belonged to motor pioneers Macrae & Dick, a 24 horse-power covered Halley, with the number ST 221. It was used mainly to transport tourists from the burgh to local beauty spots. Later, the arrival of Ford Model T, Chevrolet and other makes of chassis led to swift development in the manufacture of purpose-built buses, many throughout Britain, with bodyworks by local coachbuilders.

Thanks to W Milne for his photographs.

CROY – INVERNESS RUN

James Mackintosh of Cantraywood started to operate a bus service on alternate days between Croy and Inverness in June 1934. He can be seen inside his first bus, a 14 seater Ford, registered number ST 7657, reading his newspaper, as he awaits departure time at Farraline Park bus sttaion. He eventually sold his business to Highland Omnibuses in 1964. This photo probably dates to early post-war years, as the bus beside is a utility Guy Arab II, with basic wooden slatted seats, visible on the top deck.

REIG'S BUSES

ssing Station Square is Greig's wartime-built utility Guy Arab II, registered BST 31 and bought new in 1945. The war had almost certainly ended, as the headlamp masks, mpulsory during hostilities, had been removed, but the white markings on the mudguards, to allow pedestrians to see the vehicles in darkness, had not yet been painted over. 'illiam Greig began to run bus services in Inverness in the 1920s, but sold out in 1947 to Falkirk-based Walter Alexander & Sons, which continued operations until taken er in 1952 by the newly-formed Highland Omnibuses Ltd, part of the nationalised Scottish Bus Group. The main constituents of Highland Omnibuses itself were Highland ansport Co and Macrae & Dick.

ESSOCK FERRY RUN

e rain appears to have been belting down on this dreary day in the late 1930s, as Greig's single-decker, with a luggage rack on the roof, registered VD 3695, waited at uth Kessock pier for passengers coming off the Kessock Ferry. The car partially visible at the right is a Ford V8.

TOWN RUN

Parked on Academy Street in December 1947, in front of the former Royal Insurance building, was one of the last buses to carry the Greig's logo, a pre-war Leyland doub[le] decker registered VA 8103. The company had been acquired the previous month by W Alexander & Sons, and already the Greig's livery was rapidly being replaced [by] Alexander's blue buses.

MACRAE & DICK'S BUSES

Besides selling cars, operating a large garage and owning a fleet of taxis, Macrae & Dick also operated a significant bus service pre-war and in the early post-war years, [and] shared a Fort William service with David MacBrayne. This pristine Albion, registered ST 9200, with an Albion 26-seat body, was delivered new in May 1937. Although Macra[e] & Dick's bus operation was absorbed into the nationalised Highland Omnibuses Ltd in 1952, its garage and motor dealership is still very much to the fore in the city.

PAPER TRAIN

On a bright morning in May 1983, at No 6 Platform, Inverness Station, these men are busy preparing to load batches of Sunday papers on to the train for transport to Lairg, Sutherland, from where they would be dispatched to all corners of that sparsely-populated county. John Hay, the driver of the diesel loco hauling that particular train, sent in this picture.

ENNY FARTHING BICYCLE 1969

his rare article, on display for the camera in March 1969, failed to reach its serve price when it came up for sale at Fraser's Auction Rooms in Church reet in March 1969. Holding it up is auction room manager Jim Douglas, hile colleague Duncan Macrae is trying to keep his balance, though neither lunteered to cycle it down the street. The penny-farthing, which enjoyed a rief reign from 1870, became an icon of the Victorian era, despite the fact at it had ceased production at least 10 years before the old Queen died. This ample had come from Messrs Alex Munro's shop, which had closed shortly efore in Baron Taylor's Street, and was in original condition, apart from the edals. The only other penny-farthing to come up for auction earlier in the now ng-defunct sale rooms fetched £100. This one is thought to have been sent uth, in search of a better price.

HIGHLAND OMNIBUSES NEW FLEET
In April 1973, Highland Omnibuses became the proud owner of this fine fleet of new vehicles. Seen discussing routes for the fleet is Inspector Hamish Cameron on the left of the picture.

LAUNCHING A BOAT AT THORNBUSH
This photo, sent to us by Irene Gillespie of Old Edinburgh Road, is thought to be of a local family, the Sutherlands, launching their boat, the Heather Jane, at Thornbush while the man at the front, directing operations, is believed to be Jim Sutherland. Mrs Gillespie thinks it dates from early post-war years.

Significant Events

REFORM ACT OF 1884

Pictured in front of the Inverness Courier office are Inverness printers, lithographers and bookbinders, prior to taking part in a huge parade through the burgh to protest against an attempt by the House of Lords to prevent the passing of the Reform Act of 1884, which gave the vote to all men paying an annual rental of £10 or all those holding land valued at £10. According to local records, 20,000 people took part in the Inverness march. The man on the left, holding the horse, is James Barron, editor of the Inverness Courier. The Act was passed by a Tory Government as an appeasement measure, following a Bill introduced by the Liberals. One of the posters in the picture proclaims: "Liberals Liberating Working Classes". While this Act increased the British electorate to 5.5 million, it still left 40 per cent of adult males without the vote, and women had to wait until 1918 before those over 30 were allowed to become voters, and 1928 before full suffrage was extended to women over 21.

QUEEN VICTORIA'S DIAMOND JUBILEE

A huge crowd gathers outside Inverness Town House on 22 June 1897 to celebrate Queen Victoria's Diamond Jubilee. Those taking part, although very tightly packed together, are enjoying the event by singing in unison and listening to speeches by local dignitaries.

Local celebrations for Queen Victoria's Diamond Jubilee took place in almost every community in the United Kingdom, while it was also celebrated throughout the British Empire, when local societies, organisations and individuals got together to mark the Queen's sixtieth year on the throne. It was a time of patriotic fervour, when many monuments, community halls and buildings were erected.

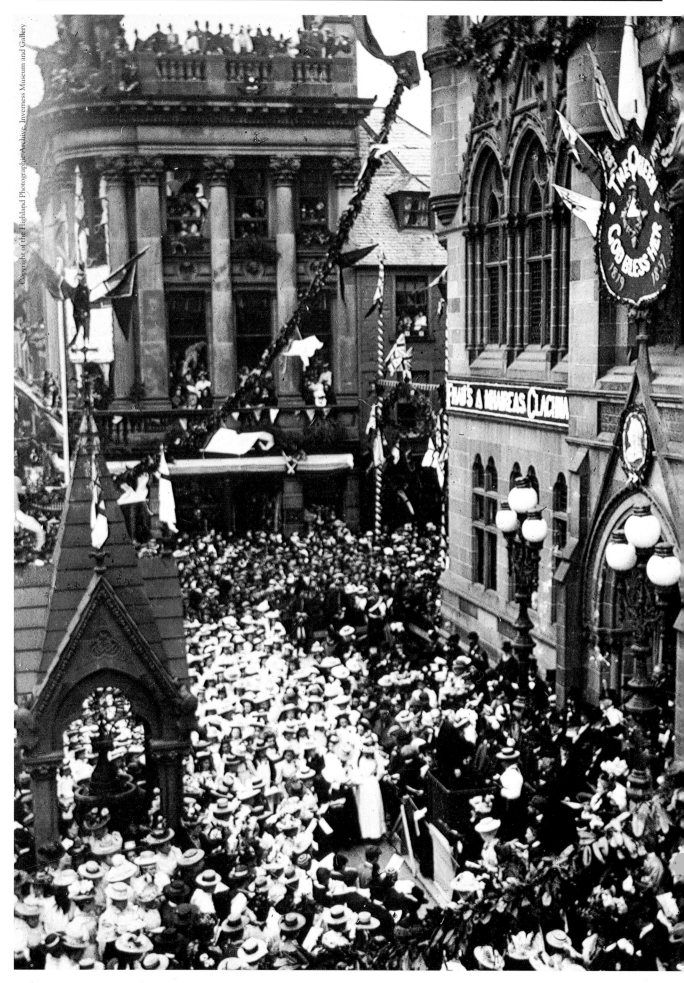

QUEEN VICTORIA'S DIAMOND JUBILEE

QUEEN VICTORIA'S DIAMOND JUBILEE – UNION STREET

This photo shows Union Street decorated to celebrate Queen Victoria's Diamond Jubilee in 1897. A Fraser & Co's store on the left made a particular effort to display its patriotism. Note the spire of the old Caledonian Hotel just beyond the other end of the street.

WINSTON CHURCHILL IN INVERNESS

Winston Churchill was still many years away from his greatest triumph, when pictured here arriving at Inverness Town House for the only cabinet meeting of the British Government ever held outside London, on 7 September 1921. Churchill was at that time Colonial Secretary, and Prime Minister David Lloyd George was on holiday at Gairloch, Wester Ross, when he learned that Ireland had rejected the King and Empire. He decided to call his Cabinet together at Inverness, rather than travel back to London, as his deputy was at Beaufort Castle and King George V at Moy. Out of this meeting arose the Inverness Formula, which created the basis of discussions on which the treaty creating the Irish Free State was agreed. The burgh council officer, William Bain, passed round a blank sheet of paper which each member signed. This is still in Highland Council's possession, and a facsimile is on display at the Town House, the original having started to fade.

Copyright of the Highland Photographic Archive, Inverness Museum and Gallery

MAIL PLANE MAIDEN FLIGHT
On 29 May 1934, at a ceremony at Longman Aerodrome, aviation pioneer Captain Ernest Edmund "Ted" Fresson received an Air Mail Pennant from the GPO's director
postal services Sir Frederick Williamson to mark the first air mail to be carried in Britain at ordinary letter rate.
Here Sir Frederick is pictured addressing a crowd which had gathered to witness this historic occasion, while Ted Fresson, in his trade-mark plus fours, waits in front of th
de Havilland Dragon, registered G-ACCE, in which shortly afterwards he inaugurated the mail service from Inverness to Kirkwall, Orkney.

Copyright of the Highland Photographic Archive, Inverness Museum and Gallery

CAPTAIN TED FRESSON
Captain Fresson is seen addressing the crowd before the maiden flight. Ted Fresson died in 1962, aged 72 and is buried in Tomnahurich Cemetery.

Copyright of the Highland Photographic Archive, Inverness Museum and Gallery

LONGMAN AERODROME
An aerial view of Longman Aerodrome in 1936, showing two carefully-mown grass runways in the form of a St Andrew's Cross, together with the hangars, seen near the trees and the perimeter road, where the main A9 highway now runs towards Kessock Bridge.

NO RAIL PRIVATISATION MARCH
This photo dates from around 1993, shortly before the Act which de-nationalised British Rail and franchised its track, rolling stock and various operational areas away to several separate private operators – at a greater cost to the taxpayer in the long run than before. Here, members of Inverness rail workshop staff are seen in High Street, prior to marching to Northern Meeting Park to protest against privatisation, and also in support of better conditions for oil platform fabrication workers at Ardersier and Nigg.

LILAC GROVE RESIDENTS' CORONATION CELEBRATIONS 1953
In this photo we return 55 years to the day in June 1953 when residents of Lilac Grove joined the rest of Britain in celebrating the Coronation of Queen Elizabeth.

FESTIVAL OF BRITAIN
Teams of runners started out from various parts of the country to celebrate the festival of Britain in 1951. Their destination was London and they were all due to converge there at the same time. The run from the north of Scotland began at John O' Groats, and took a route to Inverness before heading along the east coast to Aberdeen, then heading south. Each team had to complete three miles to a hand-over point. The Inverness team ran from the town to Allanfearn and those who were given the honour were Cpl WA McAdam, holder of the baton, with L/Cpl Tom Wilson, right, and L/Cpl John Ross. All were members of 5th Company, Boy's Brigade.

DUNAIN ROAD CHILDREN'S CORONATION PARADE 1953

Children and adults from Dunain Road are pictured here in June 1953, making their way to the Northern Meeting Park to celebrate the Coronation of Queen Elizabeth. They are being piped on their way by the late Dan Falconer, whose grand-daughter Ena Gordon passed this picture to us. Ena is the little girl in the light coat, to the left of the picture, passing a flag back to a man in the procession.

THE PAGEANT

This is a scene from a grand pageant held at the pavilion and open-air pavilion in the Ness Islands in the middle of last century, depicting some highlights in the history and legend of Inverness, including visits of Macbeth and Mary Queen of Scots, in the setting of a prefabricated castle built around the area. The lady on the right is Molly Ralph, mother of Irene Gillespie, who sent in this photo, while beside her is Margaret Taylor. Margaret's daughter Louise, now Mrs Crout, then a teenager, recalls dancing and riding a horse in the event. The commentator was Scots actor-director Calum Mill. The parts of the "castle" were taken for storage to the Northern Meeting Park, where they were used frequently as props for other events in succeeding years.

Sporting Achievements

LONGMAN GOLF CLUB

This photo shows the opening of the short-lived Longman golf course in 1895. Golf was played almost exclusively by Scots until the second half of the 19th century, and its numbers were few, the first recorded golf links, in order, being at St Andrews, Carnoustie and Dornoch. The fashion for golf expanded quickly, particularly after 1880, and on 13 November, 1883, Inverness Golf Club was formed, electing Lord Lovat as its first president. Golf courses were soon after built at Longman and Culcabock.

CROWN FOOTBALL CLUB

This was Crown football team in 1887, only two years after it took part against Nairn County in the first match to be played in the burgh under Association Football rules – a meeting which ended in a goal-less draw. The men in this photo are Hugh Macleod, S Fraser, W R Christie, F Smith, William Fraser, R Anderson, William MacKenzie, W A Campbell, R Cunningham, F Sinclair and Archie McGillivray. Crown later merged with Union – formerly Ballifeary FC – to form Inverness Thistle, and so its tradition lives on to this day.

ORSE JUMPING

ght Park was the scene of this show-jumping contest at the Northern Counties Show in 1954.

VERNESS ROVERS FOOTBALL CLUB

otball has played a very important part in the town's sporting calendar for nigh on a couple of centuries. Here we see the stalwarts of Inverness Rovers Football Club in '87. Among the players are James Dickson, W Gibb, Murdoch Macleod, Murdo Mackenzie and Abe MacKenzie.

LOVAT JUNIORS
Lovat Juniors was the youth arm of Lovat Shinty Club, founded in 1888. The team is pictured here, in the 1950s, at Bught Park, Inverness.

NORTHERN MEETING PARK PO
VAULTING
There is little information given in this ph
from Highland Council's Am Baile archi
taken in late Victorian or Edwardian da
apart from the fact that the pole-vaul
seen here at the Northern Meeting Gam
was a D Macdonald. The games, found
by the Northern Meeting Society, beca
an annual feature from 1837, with
Society founding the Northern Meet
Park in Ardross Street, the scene of t
shot, to host the event.

ANGERS' FIRST VISIT

Did this photo mark Glasgow Rangers' very first visit to Inverness, when taken at Bught Lodge, 1888, as the fledgling Glasgow football team visited the burgh? Glasgow Rangers was formed in 1872 by four Scotsmen although the name Rangers was taken from an English rugby club known to one of the founders, Moses MacNeil. The team became members of the Scottish Football Association in 1873 and moved to the Ibrox area of Glasgow in 1887, where it has since remained.

THE SWIMMER

According to Am Baile archive files, this photo shows Ian MacBain, aged 14, a member of the Inverness Swimming Team, at the South Kessock Ferry Pier in 1948, after competing with the ferry boat to cross the strait between Inverness and North Kessock. At that time, it cost six shillings to make one journey on the ferry boat. The woman in the back row, third from the right, is Mrs MacDonald, whose son Jocky MacDonald captained the Australian swimming team at the Commonwealth Games in the 1960s. He was also Inverness Champion. The man wearing a hat is Hugh Livingston, who was President of the LMS swimming club.

WINNERS OF NORTHERN COUNTIES CUP FOR GOLF 1959
This photo from the David Whyte Studios collection in the Am Baile archives, shows four very happy members of Inverness Golf Club after winning the Northern Counti
Cup in 1959. They are, from left, Dr Hamish Innes, George Calder, Taylor Bullock and Iain MacIver.

CENTRAL PRIMARY SCHOOL FOOTBALL TEAM 1957
The smiling lads shown here were members of Central Primary School's football team in 1957. They are, front, from left: - Thomson, Brian Wardrop, Alasdair MacBean, Bru
Phillips, John MacLean, John Burgess; rear, from left: George Anderson, Alister Paterson, Gael Pollitt, Keith Ballantyne, Willie Grant.

IVERNESS TECHNICAL HIGH SCHOOL AFFRIC HOUSE TEAM 1955-56

these fit young fellows made up the team of Inverness Technical High School's Affric House in 1955-56. Back row, from left: Angus MacDonald, R Ross, W Brodie, G Grant, an Greenwood, James Munro, Ronnie Lobban (reserve); front row, from left: Tommy Sutherland, Robin Gunn, Harry Smith (with ball), Victor Findlay, Alan Durham, Francis acWilliam. This photo was sent in by Christine Smith, whose husband Harry played for Inverness Caley FC during the 1960s.

IVERNESS ROYAL ACADEMY CRICKET TEAM

ctured here, around the end of World War II, are members of Inverness Royal Academy cricket team, rear, from left: unidentified, Jock - ,Billy Anderson, Mr McArdle (Latin acher), Peem Macpherson, Iain MacDonald, Hugh MacDonald (cousins); front, from left: Hamish Beauchop, Hector MacVinish, Hamish "Piggy" Gray (captain, later Lord ay of Contin), Gordon Stewart, Ian Braid, unidentified.

HILL ROVERS JUNIOR FC 1946

Members of Hill Rovers Junior FC pictured in 1946. Rear row, from left: unidentified, unidentified, Jock Shand, unidentified, Roddie Fraser, Beel Macdonald, Heck MacVinish, unidentified, Willie MacGillivray, Jock Colvin, manager and Inverness Royal Academy groundsman; front, from left: unidentified, Berty Cameron, Iain MacDona Willie Batchen, Tommy Cumming.

HIGHLAND CRICKET CLUB 1957-58

Highland Cricket Club 1957-58 at Fraser Park, while still playing in the 2nd Eleven League. Back row, from left: Alex Munro, Frank Philips, Duncan Mackay, Willie Jo Mackintosh, Eddie Grant, George Wood; front, from left: Colin Moir, Dave Christie, Jim Macpherson, Bill Anderson, Ronnie Horne, Geoff Rees.

INVERNESS HIGH SCHOOL FOOTBALL TEAM

This is the Inverness High School senior team from season 1978-79. Pictured back row from left to right are: N McLean, J MacDonald, P MacInnes, E Shand, A Chisholm, S MacKinnon. Front row, left to right are: M Lyle, S MacLaren, J MacVinish, I MacGillivray, D Young, P Waldie.

NORTH OF SCOTLAND CUP WINNERS

This celebration picture commemorates Inverness Clachnacuddin's 3-2 victory over local rivals Inverness Caledonian in the North of Scotland cup final of 1967. Pictured celebrating in style are team members Ally Chisholm, Dick Smith, Jimmy Hoge (captain), Rab Castell, Dennis Donald, Hamish Munro and Jackie Kane.

INVERNESS TECHNICAL HIGH SCHOOL 1949-50
This team from Inverness Technical High School won the Ward Trophy in session 1949-50. Team members from left, are; Rosemary MacGillivray, Ian MacBean, Marjor
Miller and Iain Cameron.

SWIMMING GALA
We haven't been given the names of these young swimmers but they're almost certainly major prizewinners in a swimming gala run by The Dairy Festival. The presence
a trophy presented by the Aviemore Centre indicates that this was probably the late 1960s or 1970s.

INTER-SCHOOL SPORTS
Overall winners of the Primary division of the Inter-school Sports in 1953, Central Primary School. Pictured back, left to right are: Mr Frank Coull, teacher, Jackie Grigor, Joan MacGillivray and Mr Fraser, headmaster. Front row, left to right are: Angus MacDonald, Doreen Macrae, Robbie MacAdam, Catherine MacGowan and Tommy Mackintosh.

ST ABBAN'S JUNIOR FOOTBALL CLUB
This photo of St Abban's Junior Football Club was snapped at the Clach Park in Grant Street in 1952. The players are, rear, from left: Billy Burns, Mike Jamieson, Archie Robertson, Donnie MacDonald, W Maclennan, Dave Munro; front, from left: Alfie Mackintosh, Peem Horne, Eddie McInnes, D Lumsden, Iain Cameron, unidentified.

CLACH RANGERS - LEAGUE CHAMPIONS

A proud moment for Clach Rangers when they won the league in 1952. Pictured are, back, left to right: G B Rodgers, L Maitland, A Patience, B Chisholm, A Chisholm, D Wyness, C Morgan. Front: J Sturrock, G Gillespie, unknown, J Robertson, S Bartlett, B Grant, B Logie.

INVERNESS Victorian Market

EST 1870

shopinverness

THE CITY in THE HIGHLANDS

The Victorian Market in the heart of the Old Town is a unique covered shopping area with 41 retail shops offering a wide variety of choice.

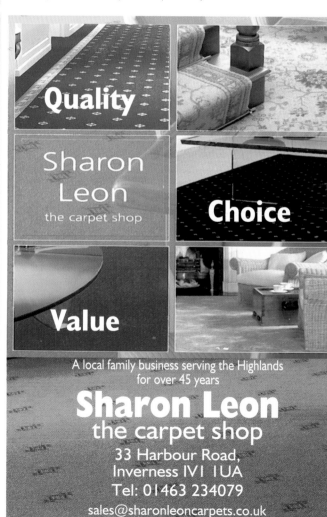

Celebrate in Style
add some Sparkle this Christmas

This year, savour the festive season to the full in magnificent surroundings. We have created a wonderful lunch menu for Christmas parties, and a very special dinner menu for evening occasions.

Pre-Christmas meals don't come any more sumptuous than this. Traditionalists can rediscover seasonal classics through the flavours of superior ingredients and cooking – a new twist on roast parsnips, Home Farm free range turkey, plum pudding with vanilla custard.

For something more avant garde, try Highland beef Carpaccio, peerless seafood and salmon from the Western Isles, or Glencalvie venison married with wild rowan berries.

Whatever you choose, you can be assured it will be prepared from the finest ingredients by some of the region's most talented chefs – call us now to make sure that Dunain Park Hotel is part of your Christmas celebrations!

Loch Ness Road, Inverness IV3 8JN
T: 01463 230512 E: info@dunainparkhotel.co.uk www.dunainparkhotel.co.uk